# Quick Guide #1 - How Top Salespeople Sell

## For new or seasoned sales professionals, managers and CEOs

I0470638

Number 1 in a series of articles by

Paul C Burr PhD

http://paulcburr.com/

# Acknowledgements

**Professor Colin Coulson-Thomas**, director, board chairman, adviser, academic, author and speaker;

**Mark Konieczko**, Founder of MKpcs.

# Contents

## The Pareto of Sales

*20% of the sales-force brings in 80% of the revenue and over 90% of the profit.*

When 'you' find out and put into common practice what your top salespeople do differently from the moderates; you raise everybody's game, including your own.

(By 'you' I mean: you, me, us, we)

———————

## Summary Bullet Points

This 30-page article (excluding appendices) bears from my research, consulting, direct selling experience and coaching within global corporations over a twenty year period. The companies I worked for directly, or in a freelance capacity with, included: IBM, Cisco, Accenture, Xerox, American Express, Standard Chartered, BP and Reckitt Benckiser.

Within you will discover how and why:

• Customers fundamentally only ask four questions:

1. *Do I trust you?*

2. *What value do you bring to the table?*

3. *Are you the right person/organisation to do business with?*

4. *How does it work (i.e. feature/benefits) or how will we work together?*

1

• Moderate performing salespeople often answer these four questions in reverse order.

• Top performers do things better and differently; they...

- Focus firstly on Questions 1 and 2

- Ask better questions that nurture insight and instil passion

- Guide customers sensitively on a spiral journey in and out of the problems they face. The dualistic nature of this journey inspires action.

- Engage the customer to evaluate the consequences of both action and inaction.

- Understand and apply what CxOs expect and value from business relationships

• Top salespeople know the answer to a CEO's first question, *"Why am I, personally, talking to you?"*

• The future of sales will rely more on truth than trust

• To raise your organisation's like-for-like sales performance by 20-30% or more

———

# Customers Ask 4 Fundamental Questions

## Illustration - 4 Questions

### 3. Are you(/is it) right for me(/us)?

Emotional: Can I see the solution working? Does it sound or feel right?

Analytical: cost, RoI, risks, timescales,

### 2. Value Understanding?

What value do you bring to the/my table?

### 4. How will it (or we) work (together)?

* Feature-benefit
* Implementation plan
* Architecture
* Design and specifications
* Service Level Agreements....

### 1. Trust?

* Personal and organisational
* Integrity and capability
* Worst case scenario
* Contract
* Technology
* Self

## Q1. Do I trust you?

If nought else, trust is the key determinant of customer loyalty. **The single biggest reason for customer disaffection is the development of a lack of trust in the relationship.**

*Three in four customers who switch out of a sales relationship do so because of a lack of trust.*

And, 'trust' is one of the two most important factors (the other being 'value') through which a customer will buy from you. Trust has a number of dimensions:

## i. Personal and organisational

Customers may trust you but not your organisation - or vice versa. As a rule of thumb it takes five times the amount of effort to gain the trust of a new customer as it does to maintain the trust of an existing customer. A well-oiled phrase: *"It can take a long time to gain the customer's trust for a large, complex solution, you're selling that is new for them - but - it takes only a second to lose that trust."*

*Tip: Make sure your intentions and behaviours focus on a win/win outcome for both you and the customer.*

## ii. Integrity

Put simply, does the customer trust that you speak the truth always? When you say you're going to do something by a given time, do you keep your word? And if something unexpected happens that takes priority over what you've committed to the customer, do you call them immediately and renegotiate the scope and/or timescale of what you promised to deliver.

*Tip: Keep your promises. Keeping agreements and commitments is the bedrock of self-trust. Self-trust is the bedrock of a 'can-do' mentality. A 'can-do' mentality is the bedrock of a 'will-do' mentality. A 'will-do' mentality goes hand in hand with passion. If you're not passionate about what you're selling, you will be giving second best. You'll be undervaluing what you sell and yourself.*

### iii. Capability

A customer might believe 100% in your integrity but may have questions about your personal (or your organisation's) capabilities to do what you say you're going to do.

At a macro-level do you have case studies and testimonies to substantiate your value proposition (ideally referencing existing, delighted and relevant household-name clients)? What research do you have that supports you or your solution's credibility?

This dimension of trust might remain unspoken about. For example, a customer executive might think, *"I believe you but I'm not convinced that you are personally capable of influencing my board of directors - which might be embarrassing for me; if I were to put you in front of them."*

*Tip: Check continually what information or reassurance your customer requires to make a decision. If you don't know, ask a direct and relevant question. For example:*

*- How comfortable do you feel about my/our/this product's capability to do the work specified?*

*- What further information do you or your board require that will give you the reassurance you require from an organisation like ours?*

*- How helpful are my questions? What am I not asking about?*

*- What else do you feel your board will want to know about my/our capability to deliver what I/we say?*

## iv. Worst-case scenario

This requires you to find out your customer's attitudes (beliefs and fears) toward failure. I once questioned the IT Director of a global household products firm about a large outsourcing deal his company had just procured from a major outsourcer. He felt his company had received a highly inspiring and competitive bid from a smaller competitor. Yet, the board went ahead with an alternative proposal because, to use his words, *"If we lie dying, covered in blood, on the road ahead, we asked ourselves 'Who do we want lying next to us?' We felt the larger company both had and would commit the extra resources necessary to sort the problem out."*

In contrast to the above example, I spoke to another IT Director who chose a small organisation deliberately - *"Because if things go wrong, we're too big a customer for them to ignore"*.

There are no rights and wrongs here. This is about the intellectual and emotional: blending the statistical elements (e.g. probability of success, risk analyses) with the customer's feelings about success and failure. Ultimately, it's about 'what-ifs' and the customer's up-front trust in you, outside of any written contract, should things not go as planned.

*Tip: There are a number scenario planning tools you can use in this instance: e.g. Future Setback Analyses, Contingency Planning, Double Learning Loops (Ref: Chris Argyris, Harvard), Pacing Strategy Before It Happens and Dashboard for Success - that (if I may plug myself) I can take you through.*

## v. Contract

Contracts specify the 'carrots and sticks' of what happens when things go right and wrong respectively. So the question asked is, *"How much faith do I place in the execution of the reward and penalty clauses in our contract, according to the eventual outcome of the sale?"*

I worked for a short while with the UK General Manager, of a global IT company, whose vision was to reduce all major client contracts to one page. I don't know whether he succeeded but I admired his ambition and the simplicity he strove for.

*Tip: Keep contracts as simple and concise as possible. Use everyday English language (before checking with your legal adviser!)*

There's a further salient question. *If either your organisation or customer is too small to sue or be sued, what's the validity of using complex and onerous contracts?*

## vi. Technology

The simple and metaphorical question a customer asks themselves is, *"Will the product or solution you propose do what it says on the tin?"*

Years ago I sold a major subsystem of new disk technology to a corporate client. Within two weeks the client started to experience availability issues and customer engineers had been called in a few times to solve the reoccurring problem. In week 3 the client called a crisis meeting. They wanted to know if we'd been having manufacturing problems.

In the run up to the meeting, I'd found out from internal sources that the new disk technology did have a problem with a very low but nonetheless unacceptable probability of occurring - and if this problem didn't manifest itself within the first six weeks of the products' lifetime, it wouldn't develop at all.

My company didn't want the issue publicised and wanted to ride out the six weeks rather than share the truth of the problem with a client. It took a fair amount of internal persuading for me to hold a meeting 'to reveal truth with the customer'. My view was: *"If the customer even suspects that we've been holding out on them then not only will we lose their trust, the customer will lose trust in our technology too - so it's not a simple matter of replacing the sales force, i.e. me! If we tell the customer the truth and the actions we have in place - that will preserve our personal and our product's integrity."* The meeting went well and within three months we got a further order.

*Tip: Truth drives out falsity, the mother of lack-of-trust. When trust, the bedrock of a relationship, crumbles you have nothing to build on.*

### vii. Self-trust

There's an old phrase: *"If you can't trust your own judgement how do/will you know you've made it correctly?"* I've known one or two CEOs personally who don't attempt to make 'big-ticket' judgements. Instead, when faced with a complex business decision, they call in independent, well-known, management consultants to recommend a decision for them. That way they have an audit trail of their compliance and governance, should things not go to plan. This tends to bring delay and adds several layers of complexity to the selling process.

If you are in dialogue with the customer before a decision is made to bring in independent advice, you have the opportunity to use the planning tools mentioned earlier (in the *Worst-case scenario* section) to explore business strategy with them.

*Tip: Simplify complexity for, and explore uncertainty with, the client. Check continually the degree of confidence the customer has in their own decision-making process.*

## Q2. What value do you bring to the table?

Let's start with CEOs, for they often have a specific question under the *'What value...'* heading. They ask themselves, *"Why am I, personally, talking to you?"* And you typically have about 15 minutes to answer that question - and raise their curiosity.

Top salespeople answer this question in a combination of ways and finish by asking permission to ask further questions. They also have a propensity to avoid explaining how they do what they do. Instead they focus on verifiable value that will grab the CEO's attention - 'the what not the how'.

### i. Corporate Identity/Capability Statement...

A concise description of the value your organisation brings to the table, that is specific enough to attract interest and broad enough to avoid you not connecting with the CEO's 'hot spot' first time.

Example, I used something like this with the CEO of a major bank: *"I heard your talk at the recent conference about the future of banking and specifically the uncertainties the industry faces. 'My company' is currently working with (CEOs of 3 global corporations) to help reduce the time to carry out their planning work by 50% and improve the quality of their decision making process by an estimated 30% as well. May I... ?"*

## ii. Personal Identity/Capability Statement...

I had the privilege of working with the top salesperson for a well known IT company in Germany. She sold into a highly specialised area of the printing industry. The management of her company and her fellow salespeople believed (a myth) that you required at least seven years experience working in the industry, as a user, to sell at the highest level with credibility. She broke the mould and dispelled the myth. She was a graduate employee with less than two years selling experience.

Her opening statement to a CxO went something along the lines of: *"I've been studying your company for two months now* (which was true)*. Specifically, I was drawn to the following statement you made about rising costs "(cites customer's quotations)". I can name two companies 'abc' and 'xyz' who have experienced problems of a similar magnitude. I have their permission to use them as a reference for the work we do. From what I've researched, I feel you could be making savings in the region of 15-30% on your cost of printing across the board BUT I can't be sure of that without some input from you. Is it ok for me to ask you some questions?"*

## iii. Seek out sources of value and fear...

From here on in, assuming you've been given the thumbs up to ask questions, your job is to seek out the major sources of value and fear. You do this by asking carefully crafted questions. I've devised a model called INCREASE[tm] to craft and evaluate questions before I ask them. I run through the INCREASE$^{tm}$ model with examples later on.

Here are two cheat sheets:

### a. What CEOs value:

The 'science' to determine value discovers what's important to the CEO. And once you understand the customer's priorities – how do you stack up (against your competitors) to deliver against them?

Here are sources of value (business drivers and problems to fix) that CEOs look for:

• Cash – *Will your proposal improve our cash position?*

• Cost Down – *Will we reduce costs?*

• Revenue/Market Share Up – *Will we make competitive gains?*

• Agility/Speed – *Can we move, reshape, transcend quickly?*

• Security – *Will we be better protected?*

• Governance – *Am I compliant with Company Law?*

• Product/Service/Cost Leadership – *Will our own customers notice and value the changes in our organisation that your proposal offers?*

• Innovation (e.g. Technology, New Business Models) – *Do I want (to be seen) to be first in the marketplace, to do something differently? Does your proposal accelerate the process?*

• Personal Credibility – *Can I use your proposal to advance my own prospects and standing?*

• People – *Will your proposal raise the effectiveness and job satisfaction of people?*

• Something else? – If you don't know, ask *"What else do you feel is important for me to know?"* Even if you feel you know, ask anyway.

Put concisely, you need to understand profoundly what's important in the hearts and minds of CEOs and convey the value you bring to the table in their language, not yours.

At this stage you may have provided sufficient verifiable value for the CEO to progress the sale. And there's often a temptation to press on. In doing so, you may miss another, often unspoken, factor that weighs heavily in the CEO's mind (as well as most of us) - fear.

Top performers are more 'savvy' about how to approach the challenges a CEO faces. Here's an extract from a blog I wrote:

### b. What CEOs fear:

*The more you earn a customer's trust, the more fears they share with you. They give you more power deliberately to help them.*

My thanks go to Professor Colin-Coulson Thomas who shared with me the bounty of a minute fraction of his wisdom, and made a significant contribution to the following list.

CEOs fear:

• Bad earnings news: the most likely and quickest sign of departure.

• Corporate programs don't deliver: mergers and acquisitions *"achieve 70% of their potential"* at best.

• Failure to turnaround ailing sales quick enough.

• Change takes too long: 'Corporate Firewalls' prevent people from getting it done.

• Investors don't understand: a CEO spends 40% of their time articulating strategy and some argue that's not enough.

• Personal wealth at risk: e.g. missed deadlines can lead to private investors swallowing up the shareholding of a company

• Lack of innovation: playing it safe is no longer an option these days. Competitors and customers are moving too quickly.

• Talent gaps in performance: e.g. (cited earlier) *"20% of the sales-force bring in 80% of the revenue..."*

• Conflict in the boardroom: too much time spent looking inwards leaves too little time to focus on the customer.

• Personal credibility at risk: any of the above means less likelihood of stepping up the ladder of success and/or lack of a legacy of note. These in turn can lead to...

• Personal health at risk: where the stressed mind-body connection can have serious consequences. I know of one CEO who, after missing targets set by investors, developed terrible eye problems because he didn't like what he saw. Another developed disabling back pain through a lack of self-esteem. Another who was deemed too rigid and inflexible developed problems with their joints.

By this stage you may well have established trust in, and the worthiness of, your value proposition BUT further work will be needed to answer Question 3 below - and inspire action. The customer may be very interested or even convinced. Now your task is to encourage them to commit - i.e. sign the sales contract.

## Q3. Are you the right person/organisation to do business with?

This 'big question', the answer to which makes or breaks the sale has two dimensions to it, *Intellectual* and *Emotional*.

### i. Intellectual

This is essentially the business case for your proposal. What are the costs? What are the RoI, payback period and other financial measures? What are the risks? What contingencies exist (and so on)? I'll focus on the cost or price of your solution.

**Illustration - Price Competitiveness: Bandwidth**

Lack of value
and possibly
lose trust

⬆

Maximum

### Success!

Minimum

⬇

Lose trust in
capability or
integrity

Price competitiveness succeeds in a bandwidth, within acceptable tolerance limits. If your price is too high, in comparison to your competitors, the customer may think you are trying to pull a 'fast one'. They might question the trust they put in you.

I was working with a European domestic products firm who were evaluating proposals to integrate the IT, of a company they were in the process of merging with, into a single infrastructure. One 'very big' vendor's quotation was 50% higher than the maximum the buyer had expected (their upper tolerance limit) and 60% higher than the next highest quotation. The buyer's trust in the 'very big' company came into question. Next, when the highest bid vendor reduced its prices in line with that of the second highest bidder: all the customer trust the 'very big' vendor had earned to date went out the window - 'no sale this or next time'.

Price also has a lower bandwidth: the lowest price a customer expects to pay. If your price falls below this level, you might invoke the customer to start questioning the quality of your product, solution or human resources. You might also unwantingly encourage the customer to ask themselves if they think you're buying their business at a loss deliberately, to tie them in.

Let us return and assume you have a highly competitive, if not the best, business case amongst your competitors. Does the customer feel it is compelling?

Feeling 'compelled' is an emotion, not a thought. And feelings dwell in your body whereas thoughts occur in the mind. You may have a sound intellectual business case but you require the heart as well as the mind of the buyer to win the sale. **It is thus the answers you give to customer's next questions where the sale is won or lost.**

## ii. Emotional

Let's assume you have gained the customer's trust and have agreement with them over your value proposition. The customer now asks of themselves: *Can I see your proposition working in my organisation? Does the proposition, feel right? Does it look right? Does it ring true?* (And perhaps even more obscurely depending on how the customer prefers to process feelings through their five senses) *Does it smell or taste sweet?*

Let's further assume that the customer answers 'yes' to your solution now being the right one. It still leaves the question, *Is it compelling?*

The process of making your proposal compelling starts as you build your value proposition (Question 2) and completes its journey here.

Consider a complex sales solution that purports to solve a number of customer business issues, some of which may have been unknown to the customer before you started selling to them.

Top salespeople do three things to inspire and raise the customer's conviction to act; they:

1. Break down the myriad of customer business opportunities and issues into manageable chunks.
2. Discern with the customer those existing and potential issues that can be controlled or influenced from those (perhaps unknowns) that need to be guarded against.

3. With the customer's agreement, they take the customer into each manageable-chunk-sized opportunity or problem and out again. They may do this several times. Why?

Each time a customer crosses the boundary between sitting in the feeling of having a problem and then sitting in the comparative feeling of having the problem go away - they begin to visualise not only their 'pain' disappearing but also new opportunities that arise in the 'problem-solved picture'.

Likewise, when the customer sits repeatedly in the feeling of a lost-opportunity (i.e. the consequences of doing nothing) versus the feeling of achieving that opportunity - they become more and more compelled to take that opportunity (i.e. buy your solution).

*Tip: At each stage of the value generation process to make your solution compelling in the eyes of the customer, always leave the customer in a more positive frame of mind - i.e. the prospect of a problem solved or an opportunity taken.*

Taking the customer in and out of opportunities and problems is an acquired skill. Care needs to be taken not to overdo it. You gauge this over time by checking with the customer continually if they are getting what they want from the sales process.

Let's go back to the CEO. Let's assume you've built the trust along with the best and most compelling value proposition. As the buying process comes to a decision, the CEO will confer with their people about the technical/implementation quality or legal compliance of your solution.

This requires that you have simultaneously answered Question 4 below with those people who have a say or an interest in the technical and detailed aspects of your proposal. Timing is important.

The CEO now has the concurrence of their people about the viability of your proposal. You've got the timing right so that they feel compelled to proceed - what next?

Here lies a little observation. Top salespeople rarely do more than simply ask for the order because the customer has the information they need, the time is right, and they feel compelled to say 'yes'. Quite often, in such instances, top salespeople don't need to close the sale; the customer closes it for them.

## Q4. How does it work (i.e. features - benefits) or how will we work together?

This is where moderate performers usually feel most comfortable. I'll explain some of the reasons why later.

You spend most of your time answering questions in this category to those who will implement your proposal and those whose daily life will be affected by it.

Under Question 4 you'll be answering questions on details, features and benefits, for example:

• Changes to working practices

• Technical, structural and architectural specifications

• Implementation plans

• Service Level Agreements

• Contractual details - and so on...

Whilst it is equally important to get the technical or detailed recommendation flowing upwards to the CEO, I won't spend too much time here because this is the area that most salespeople spend most of their time - and thereby hangs a flaw in how many salespeople are trained.

Tip: *When a CEO says "Yes, I'll go with it," what they probably mean is "Yes, I'll go with your solution when my people recommend it to me".*

---

## Turning Sales Outside In

I find most salespeople, especially in technology companies, are trained to sell 'inside out' - i.e. *"Here's your problem/opportunity", "Here are the implications" (find the problem and make it worse), "Now here's a product and here's its features", "Here's the benefit to each feature", "Here's the business case"* (plus a few more logical arguments/techniques to handle objections etc) *"So will you buy?"* Much sales training follows this kind of sequence - and there's more.

Technology companies tend to use their most 'techy' people to design sales product training. The 'techies' are very proud of the technology they've developed and rightly so. They can wax lyrically about all the features of their products and the benefits these features bring. It's then a simple case of morphing feature-benefits into a business case - job done? No.

I was interviewing a 'top-salesperson' about how useful his company's (a well known global IT corporation) training material was, for a recently launched advanced technology into the UK market. He answered that everything was there except it was 'inside-out' and 'back to front'. I asked him to explain how he would advise his colleagues to go about selling the new technology/solution like he had done.

*"This 'solution', although slightly complex at first, is world class and still new to UK market. So first you need to educate the customer in the generics of the value that this sort of solution brings, namely: cost reduction, lower management and technical manpower overheads, better security and certificated compliance according to EU governance laws. It took me a day of 'white-boarding' with my technical support people to get the story right (i.e. compelling).*

*Secondly, to back this up, we already have over 1000 blue chip American companies using this technology to great effect. We have a lot of evidence to reassure my client that this new technology works in organisations of the same size, complexity and stringent governance practices as theirs.*

*Thirdly, you can then press home the unique advantages of my company's solution over anyone else's. By this point, the customer is not only sold on the concept as workable in their organisation but also buys into our unique value proposition.*

*Doing a straight 'feature/benefit sell' may be ok when you're selling to techies, but at Board level you've got to 'keep the picture big'."*

The sales 'storyline' above focused on value and earning trust so well that the client thereafter worked out the business case collaboratively with the salesperson; to underpin the picture they already had in their mind of the £several-hundred-thousand solution working in their organisation.

The feature/benefit equation did come into the storyline but only after the customer was inspired and curious to know, *"So why are you (and your solution) best for us?"* And the answer to that question, in this successful example, came third.

---

## Questions that INCREASE^(tm) Wisdom and Inspire Action

The old phrase, *"You have two ears and one mouth, use them in that ratio",* provides good advice; mix two parts listening to one part speaking. But there's another level. When you speak, you either ask a question or you advocate. And selling is about getting the mix right as the customer's buying process evolves.

The more clearly you understand the customer's aspirations and fears (which can change as their buying process evolves), the better you equip yourself to respond.

Top salespeople question continually not just where a customer is intellectually (logic and reasoning) in their thinking but also where the customer is emotionally (feelings, e.g. intentions, motivation, confidence, fears).

Let me reiterate, this is about asking questions with integrity to genuinely understand the customer better. You can self-assess your integrity 'in-flight' by first understanding, before articulating with the customer, your reasons for asking a specific question. The more powerful the question you ask, the wiser you become as to the sensibility of what's going on in the customer's mind and body, especially what's going on below the surface.

Here's an acronym I evolved to design key questions that INCREASE[tm] knowledge, insight and wisdom for both you and the client.....

**I**nsightful - Might the question get the customer to look at a problem or opportunity differently?

**N**ew - Is the customer used to answering this question without having to think much? (In both this and the previous question, a fresh perspective unearths wisdom to the client and you.)

**C**oncise - Does it get the customer to focus on one thing at a time? (And thereby avoid the customer from seeing something as too big or complex to contemplate.)

**R**elevant - Will the customer see its connection to the issue under discussion? (Or might I have to guide them there with one or more intervening questions?)

**E**xpress feelings - Does the question ask the customer their feelings, or how they see something or how it sounds? (We do things for two reasons: out of passion or fear, both of which are feelings not thoughts.)

**A**nalyse - does the question probe the customer about the reasoning and logic they use? (This reinforces the validity of the answer the customer comes up with because it's their logic and reasoning, not yours. It also increases your sensibility as to where 'they are at'.)

Speculate - does the question get the customer to answer the question *"What if...?"* or *"What might happen if...?"* (Used tactfully, these types of question evoke passion and fears that will ultimately determine the customer's inspiration to act sooner rather than later or do nothing.)

Evaluate - does the question get the customer to put a value on/to something? (The answer to this question not only reveals the quality of the business case in the customer's mind but also emotional attachment (passion or fear) they have to an outcome.

*Tip: Focus on the key factors that represent the most important areas of gain/pain to the customer.*

As you formulate a question, ask yourself, how well does it meet all the criteria embedded within INCREASE[tm]?

Here are some example questions I use, when meeting a client for the first time, once I have their permission to ask *"a small number of questions I've prepared in advance, so I can (hopefully) then put better words, to anything I want to say, into your context? Is that ok?"*

My questions are fairly generic and can be adapted to a niche context. Mine, for example, is coaching. They also help you find out how important the niche, that you're in, is in the customer's mind, within the total picture of their business priorities.

I've added some subliminal language 'commands' in brackets that deserve a separate article in their own right. Such subliminal instructions connect with customer's unconscious mind to set its thinking wheels in motion because it operates a might faster than the conscious mind.

You don't have to use the words in brackets but you might want to experiment with them in a safe environment to explore their effectiveness:

• *(As you think about the full range of responsibilities your role demands...) What do you feel are the two or three most important aspects of your role, right now?*

• *(So as you look into the future...) Over and above key performance measures, how will you know if you are being successful in say, 'n' months time?*

• *(And coming back to the present...) What are the major changes going on within or outside your company, right now, and how do they affect you?*

• *Over and above everything you've said so far, what's working well and what isn't? Where would you specifically like to see improvement?*

• *And as you think about everything you've said so far, what do you feel is your number one priority?*

• *May I play back to you, what seem to be the key points - so that I haven't missed out, or got the wrong slant, on anything I heard you say?*

Assuming you've engaged the customer in all the questions above, you should now have a much richer understanding of the customer's passions and fears AND....

• Brought new insights to the surface for the client such that they feel inspired.

• By the nature of your questions, the customer knows you appreciate what's important to them.

• The customer may well give you permission to focus further on their priorities - be it more questioning or engage in your other task, that of advocating.

———

## Create Compelling Messages

I haven't come up with a simple acronym yet to remember all the factors below. So I suggest you work through them sequentially.

Ask yourself:

• *What do I wish to advocate?* Covers the options the customer has, including 'doing nothing'.

• *What is my storyline?* The 'trail' grounded in today's reality that leads to a vision of the future.

• *Is my storyline...* (Checklist: go for as many of these items as you can.)

    1. *Customer-centric?*

        - Specifies tangible business value

        - Generates reassurance

    2. *Concise?* It focuses on what's of most importance to the customer

    3. *Articulate?*

        - Simplifies complexity by breaking things down into manageable chunks

        - Connects the dots of everything that's important in the eyes of the customer

- Delineates between what's known and unknown

4. *Unique?* In terms of the value it brings

5. *Compelling?* Addresses the topmost passions and fears held by the customer

6. *Insightful?* Gets the customer to re-categorise their view point so that:

- They see something they seek in a new light or...

- Rings new bells in their ears or...

- Develop a new feeling for what's possible or better still...

- They feel inspired to act or do something differently

7. *Broad* enough to capture many people's interest and *specific* enough to advocate what you are focusing on?

8. *Based on facts, logic and reason* - as well as the *emotional* aspects of the customer's decision making process?

9. *Simple?* Enough so that the customer feels motivated and competent to spread your message on your behalf to other stakeholders in their organization

———

# Top Salespeople in the Future will Forge Truth...

The higher up a corporate customer's management hierarchy you call, the more uncertainty there is to deal with. At operational levels, you deal with business unit managers who, by and large, are all measured against the same tangible yardsticks of performance.

Once above that level you deal with leaders of change who, by definition, are looking to do things that haven't been done before. They focus on defining and creating new realities. They are the 'harbingers' of tomorrow's world.

The 'harbingers' delve into the unknown. Their task is becoming increasingly difficult because the unknown, aided and abetted by ever increasing changes in technology, is getting larger and darker. There's much more data about what's going on but can it be extrapolated with confidence into the future?

*There is very little data that accurately measures what the world or business may look like in anything beyond six weeks hence.*

I went to series of banking seminars in and around mid 2008. Were there 'green shoots' appearing in the economy? Were we in an elongated dip? Were we starting a 'double dip'? Nobody could predict accurately. Any form of optimism was mooted very cautiously. More data was called for. More analyses were completed. Did they make any of the forecasts more believable? No. Bankers and politician's couldn't predict the future with any sense of accuracy. They/we still can't.

*We live with more data, more unknowns and more uncertainty than we ever have because the future happens a lot more quickly than it used to.*

The more uncertainty faced, the more we need to put trust in our advisors and ourselves. But trust is not truth.

*Trust is the gap between what we know and what we put our faith in.*

Here lies the role for, dare I say, a 'newish' generation of salespeople. There was a biggish fad a few years ago to develop salespeople to become 'trusted expert advisors'. My personal experience is that you can count on one hand the number of 'broad-based industry experts' in, for example, a global IT sales organisation who know as much about, say, banking as the bankers themselves. And even then you might find you have three or more of your fingers missing.

The new sales role is more than mentoring and different. The relationship with the customer still requires a huge amount of trust but the 'new salesperson' doesn't need to be an industry expert. Instead, they develop the expertise to help explore uncertainty and find answers in the hidden nooks and crannies of the psyche of their customers' organisation.

By psyche, I mean the intellectual and emotional capabilities of its leaders and workforce. These salespeople don't have magical answers. Instead, they have magical questions that spark the customers imagination into collaboratively putting together a believable 'image-in-ions'.

This is about making the sales/customer relationship equation: 1 + 1=3. The sum of the parts is more than

28

each party can bring to the table on their own. But this is a relationship that transcends trust, it's rooted in truth. There are no hidden agendas.

*When you exchange truth with another wholly, you no longer need to trust them. What remains is your trust in yourself.*

This is more than being an 'honest broker'. The salesperson of the future will still bring skills and know-how of their own industry to the table. BUT, the top salesperson will be an intrepid explorer too; capable of guiding clients into the unknown and back again safely. They achieve this by knowing how to find and help release that which holds the client back, namely fear.

*Only four things hold us back in life: shame, anger, sadness and fear. When you look inside these negative emotions, you discover they're all fear. The opposite of truth is falsity. Behind all falsity lies fear.*

The top salesperson earns the customer's trust because they deal in truth, and only truth. Truth drives out falsity which ultimately releases fear. More than trust, truth forges a relationship that can connect to the 'greater good' for all involved.

*A business world forged by relationships rooted in truth might be a pipe dream. But we have to imagine it before we can create it. As we look back over history and specifically the world economy over last few years, it begs the question, "What sustainable alternative do we have?"*

# Thank you...

...For purchasing this article. I plan to write further 10-15 page business articles in this Quick Guide series. The next has the working title, *Quick Guide II: Learn How to Spot, Mimic and Become a Top Salesperson.*

If you'd like further information about the variety of services I engage in, please visit these websites:

http://paulcburr.com ~ extensive and ethereal blog-site that combines business and ancient wisdom

http://www.facebook.com/PaulCBurr ~ **Beowulf** has over 14,500 followers

http://twitter.com/paulburr

www.cotoco.com ~ for 'wisdom- transfer' solutions

or

mailto: doctapaul@paulcburr.com

———

## Appendix 1: How to Achieve 20-30% or More Sales Growth from your Existing Sales Organisation

For decades, conventional sales training hasn't changed that much. I've known some large organisations who have spent millions of dollars rolling out bespoke, detailed and corporate account sales methodologies. Did they make a return on their investment? The benchmark figures, I've seen, reveal a 5-15% increase in sales at best. All along, there was another way of achieving higher sales growth.

I often ask my clients to ponder a phrase:

*"You already have the answer to every question you ask of yourself."*

Thus, the role of a non-expert coach is to help the client ask the right questions. And I suggest, rather than going outside and investing vast sums on sales methodologies; these global organisations could have asked:

*"What is it that our top tier salespeople do differently from the rest? And how can we transfer the what (and how), they do things differently, to everyone?"*

Wisdom is knowledge plus the willpower and know-how of when to apply that knowledge. Widespread 'wisdom transfer' equips everyone to copy what your top performers do. 'Wisdom-transfer' is not 'skills transfer'; it's more, much more. It involves the transfer of your top-performers' confidence, motivation and sense of timing, as well as their skills. Rapid 'wisdom-transfer' requires a different approach that transcends the conventional approach to skills training.

Conventional trainers will say, and believe, that they can transfer wisdom easily. They can't, period, but they don't find this out until they've, by and large, failed. (It takes months, if not years, to reconcile this, assuming the original decision hasn't been swept under the carpet. In the meantime a huge opportunity has been postponed.)

> *Conventionalists fail because they don't know that they don't know how.*

Building a rapid 'wisdom-transfer' system requires a different mindset that deploys a new approach in design.

> *'Transferring the wisdom' rapidly of your top tier salespeople, to others, creates a spiral growth in sales.*

Imagine a large sales organisation. For every ten salespeople, you'll have two at the top end of the sales curve of performance, six moderates and two low performers. The moderates (and low performers for that matter) increase their sales performance because they are able to copy precisely what the top tier do. As this happens, imagine a spiral effect - that by some quirk - the top tier increases its sales performance too - so that the moderates subsequently have higher performance techniques to copy. A spiral in sales growth starts to loop between the top and middle sales tiers, again and again. Now you've imagined this spiralling phenomenon, what does it take to make it a reality? And why does it happen?

When you isolate, simplify and share what top salespeople do (= 'wisdom transfer') there are financial, practical, design and political considerations:

1. The top salespeople's aggregate sales go up. Why?

 • Many of the things top salespeople do well, they do from knowledge that is tacit or intuitive. Once their collective wisdom is spelt out for one and all, the top performers, by and large, will pick up and apply the aggregate of their pool of knowledge straight away.

 • Top salespeople are metaphorically like modern jazz musicians; they are naturally curious and willing to experiment with the unknown. When what they do intuitively or tacitly is made clear to them, they take that as the base line of their approach to selling and then see how far they stretch the boundaries further.

2. If you can raise your top salespeople's current sales contribution (which makes up 80% of your current revenue) by 30% - then your total like for like sales revenue increases by (30% of 80% =) 24%.

This doesn't mean that you only raise a corresponding increase of 6% in total revenue (=30%-24%) from the moderate performers. Their journey ahead and the methods they use are already proven in the field. The 'ex-moderates' that nurture their motivation and confidence, as a result of using the 'wisdom-transfer' tools, can go on to achieve much higher proportional gains.

3. Top performers are highly motivated, confident and competent, the moderates less so. The 'wisdom transfer,' from top to lower tiers of salespeople, flows well when it is rapid and simple; so that it raises

others' motivation and confidence as well as their competence.

New developmental design techniques combined with distribution technology, along with a different mindset, make the difference between success and failure.

4. How rapid? What used to take days of skills transfer can now be transferred in minutes. I've observed how, using a bespoke 'app', the transferral of sixty minutes of 'top salespeople's wisdom' has been more effective than three days of conventional classroom training and reinforcement.

5. How do you keep new wisdom circulating? By automating the 'wisdom distribution process', your whole sales-force is as up to date as possible with the latest questions, messages, case studies and any other collateral that your top salespeople have come up with.

6. Such a revolutionary 'wisdom transfer' programme requires executive sponsorship to oversee new collaborative working practices. This may not be that simple to obtain if your organisation's existing training and development department doesn't carry a high enough status on the day to day, boardroom agenda.

7. Successful 'wisdom-transfer' becomes a 'living agenda' when the sales-force accept responsibility for its part in the upkeep of transfer system's content - week in, week out. (There are those who say they are already doing 'wisdom transfer' but when you look under the covers, they are not. There is a simple acid test to check how well the training material available is 'woven into the fabric' of the sales organisation. Ask the sales force how often they use and contribute to the sales training material available.)

## Summary Remarks...

There is a huge opportunity for organisations, that want to 'pave the way in wisdom transfer', to get ahead of the wave of how their industry contemporaries develop their sales force to sell.

Rapid 'wisdom-transfer' requires a mindset change to, as well as a skill-set change in, your approach to sales development. Furthermore, it requires collaborative executive sponsorship to forge a close, if not seamless, working relationship between departments (in this instance: sales, sales operations, marketing, IT and training). The higher rewards make the collaborative effort worth your while, I suggest!

*Instead of 5-15% growth (the bandwidth of conventional sales training), you're looking at 20-30%, possibly more, in like-for-like sales growth.*

Author's interest: I'm a Non-executive Director of Cotoco Ltd, who specialise in 'wisdom-transfer' designs and technologies. The transfer techniques can be applied in any organisational function.

---

# Appendix 2: About me, Paul C Burr

Photo © Stephen Cotterell

I'm in the business of equipping people to improve their effectiveness by 30%+ in a matter of weeks, sometimes days.

Business Client: *"I have worked with Paul periodically over the past 8 years to gain solutions to a number of people issues / opportunities. If you are looking for a Personal Coach to make a High Performer / High performing Team even better (particularly a senior player) – I would not hesitate to recommend him." -* Sandra Ventre, Management Development Director, Reckitt Benckiser (now with Qantas)

Private Client: *"You have been so instrumental in the positive changes in my life, I set quite a few goals, and one by one my goals are being achieved, thanks to you, showing me how." -* Debbie (via Skype) Cape Town, South Africa.

**The Skills and Passions in Me**

*Life doesn't get better by chance; it gets better by change. And change is a journey that's two parts, emotional, to one part, intellectual.*

Most of us don't achieve what we set out to achieve at the first attempt. If the outcomes you sought were down to a purely intellectual exercise then you would have achieved them already - would you not? Whether you're a top or moderate performer (or underperforming right now) - every change you make in life is a journey, two parts emotional to one part intellectual. We are twice as likely to hold ourselves back because of self-imposed emotional blocks as opposed to intellectual problems. Put simply, I equip people to tackle challenging emotional journeys.

Corporate clients use me as a 'business coach', personal clients probably see me as more of an 'energy healer'. In both cases I help clients to release the emotional blocks so that they cultivate and apply their innate willpower, imagination, courage and creativity to achieve the business and personal outcomes they seek.

I've over thirty five years of 'b2b' corporate sales and management experience, fifteen years of which overlap with my business and personal coaching work. I've a PhD in Statistics and a First Class Honours Degree in Mathematics. I'm qualified as a *Master Practitioner* in: NLP, this/past life regression and hypnotherapy.

I write books, blogs and have just started a series of business articles based upon my own original research, experience and observations in corporate and SME business.

I study and practice ancient wisdom, astrology, casting runes, dowsing, the I Ching and the Tarot.

I love listening to music – rock, jazz, country... you name it. I sing a bit too.

I'm a passionate football fan of Newcastle United Football Club, in "Geordieland", in The North-East of England.

**My Promise:**

*The material I use is powerful, very powerful. I know of nothing quicker or more effective. It's non-mainstream - which means you get non-mainstream results*

.

**The Author in Me**

*Learn to Love and Be Loved in Return*

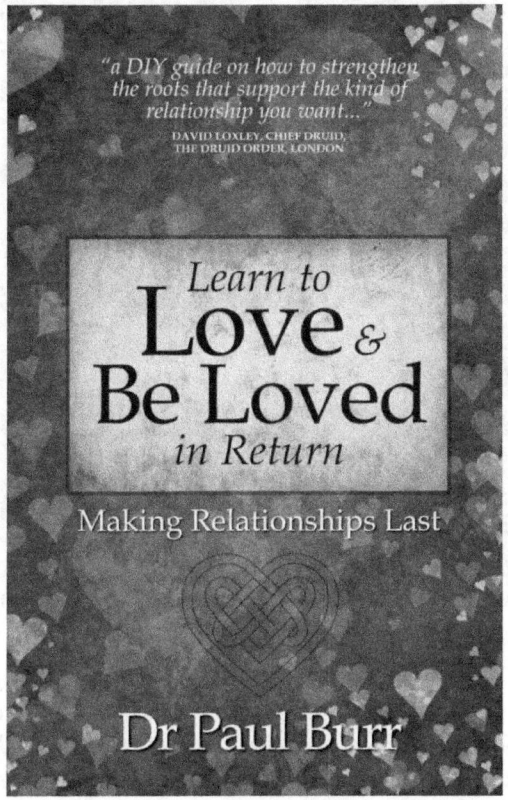

"*Uplifting: this is one of those books that arrives in your life at just the right time, when you need it most. The author is able to convey a very deep and meaningful message in an easy to read and understand format with a step by step guide on how to achieve this. The best type of love is unconditional and what better place to start than with yourself.*" -
Rhedd (Amazon reviewer)

*2012: a twist in the tail*, a novel with spiritual insights

*"This is a compelling story for our troubled times. Paul C Burr writes with passion and compassion about moral uncertainties and the quest for salvation and spiritual fulfilment. Go with the flow, trust your inner-self and enjoy this humane and optimistic tale."* - Professor John Ditch, York, UK

*"This is a gripping read - beautiful, insightful and very enjoyable. I found phrases and thoughts staying with me, and becoming part of my understanding of the world."* - Caroline Eveleigh, Getting to Excellent

**Defrag your Soul**

*"You should be proud of DYS Paul. I think it is amazing and I'm still thinking hard about what you've written."* - Amanda Giles, Author

*"DYS whispered to me, 'take heart, be aware, let your journey this far nourish your inner self to be at peace, to love and to shine as your journey continues'."* - Penelope Walsh, Book Review

## The Blogger in Me

I host a number of Facebook pages that have amassed an aggregate of over 20,000 followers. The most popular page, **Beowulf**, links to extracts from my works as well as the words from others who inspire me.

My blogs cover a broad number of topics to help you in your personal and business life. The 'wisdom' shared comes from what I pick up from day to day life, my research and my client work.

Thank you for your consideration.

/|\

Paul C Burr PhD

http://paulcburr.com

www.ingramcontent.com/pod-product-compliance
Lightning Source LLC
Chambersburg PA
CBHW071542170526
45166CB00004B/1515